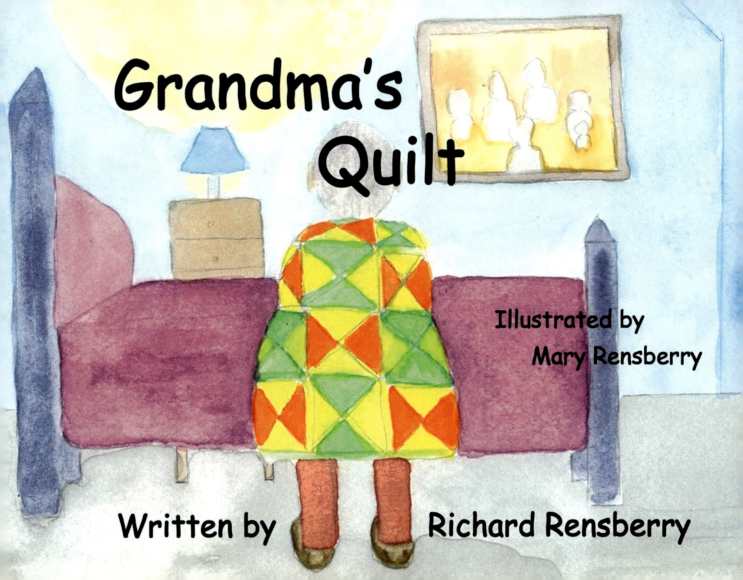

Copyright © 2017, Richard Rensberry

All rights reserved.

No part of this publication may be reproduced, stored in a retrieval system or transmitted in any form or by any means electronic, mechanical, photo-copied, recorded or otherwise, without the prior written permission of the publisher and authors.

Published by: QuickTurtle Books LLC®

http://www.richardrensberry.com

ISBN: 978-1-940736-40-2
Published in the United States of America

This book is dedicated to
master quilter, Cleta Troyer,
of Fairview, Michigan,
who has quilted and donated
so many beautiful quilts to the
Mennonite Relief Sale.

If I were grandma's quilt,
I'd hold you close and snug

as a teddy bear like Dad's heartfelt bedtime hug.

If I were grandma's quilt,
I'd wrap you in my soul's
warm and blissful yellow,
red and blue rainbows.

If I were grandma's quilt,
no cold would touch your heart,
no blizzard chill could steal
nor make my arms depart.

If I were grandma's quilt,
I'd hold you tight and snug
as a teddy bear like Mom's
heartfelt bedtime hug.

If I were grandma's quilt,
I'd be your closest friend,
I'd be there night and dawn
and again at daylight's end.

If I were grandma's quilt,
the dark would acquiesce
to dreams of little girls
and boys in pajama dress.

If I were grandma's quilt,
I'd hold you tight and snug
as a teddy bear like Dad's
heartfelt bedtime hug.

If I were grandma's quilt,
the wind would softly sigh,
take its icy breath
and blow so lightly by.

If I were grandma's quilt,
we'd smell of hollyhocks,
of rosebuds born of June
and blossoms of the phlox.

If I were grandma's quilt,
I'd hold you tight and snug
as a teddy bear like Mom's
heartfelt bedtime hug.

The End

Rhyme for Young Readers Glossary

1. blissful- very happy
2. blizzard- windy winter storm
3. dawn- sunrise in the morning
4. acquiesce- agree to quietly
5. hollyhocks- large and sweet smelling flowers
6. phlox- showy flowers

More books in the Rhyme for Young Readers Series by QuickTurtle Books®

If I Were A Heart
If I Were A Caterpillar
If I Were A Garden
If I Were A Book
If I Were A Lighthouse
Big Ships
I Wish It Were Christmas
Abigail's Chickens
Monster Monster
Goblin's Goop
How the Snake Got Its Tail
Colors Talk